Sports Illustrated KIDS

BASEBALL'S
GREATEST
NICKNAMES

Babe, Hammerin' Hank,
Mookie, and More!

by
THOM STORDEN

CAPSTONE PRESS
a capstone imprint

Capstone Captivate is published by Capstone Press, an imprint of Capstone.
1710 Roe Crest Drive
North Mankato, Minnesota 56003
capstonepub.com

Library of Congress Cataloging-in-Publication Data is available on the Library of Congress website.
ISBN: 978-1-6639-0683-0 (hardcover)
ISBN: 978-1-6639-2039-3 (paperback)
ISBN: 978-1-6639-0680-9 (ebook pdf)

Summary: Many of the greatest baseball players have earned funny, odd, or interesting nicknames during their careers. Read to find out the stories behind baseball's legendary nicknames.

Image Credits
Alamy: Archive World, 17, Niday Picture Library, 11; Associated Press: 22, 24, Curtis Compton/Atlanta Journal-Constitution, 16, Harold Filan, 20, Harry Harris, 19, Rene Johnston, 27, Rusty Kennedy, 25; Getty Images: Bettmann, 29, Frank Lennon, 26; Library of Congress: George Grantham Bain Collection, 12; Shutterstock: Dusty Cline, Cover, Frank Romeo, 4, Tiwat K, (doodles) design element throughout; Sports Illustrated: Al Tielemans, 10, Erick W. Rasco, 8, 9, 15, John W. McDonough, 6, Robert Beck, 14, Walter Iooss Jr., 23; Wikimedia: Jefferson R. Burdick Collection, 28

Editorial Credits
Editor: Erika L. Shores; Designer: Terri Poburka; Media Researcher: Morgan Walters; Production Specialist: Laura Manthe

All internet sites appearing in back matter were available and accurate when this book was sent to press.

All records and statistics in this book are current through the 2020 season.

Printed and bound in the United States of America. PO4270

TABLE OF CONTENTS

Words in **BOLD** are in the glossary.

Nicknames of the Diamond

Baseball players might be the most nicknamed in all of sports. Players have had animal nicknames such as Rabbit, Rats, Big Cat, and Wonder Dog. Other players were Muddy Chicken, Swamp Fox, and Lizard King. That's just for starters. Along with animal nicknames, baseball has rhyming nicknames, playful nicknames, and funny nicknames.

Baseball games are played in stadiums. They are also called ballparks. This photo shows the Rangers' ballpark in Texas.

Diamond Fact

Another name for a baseball field is a diamond. The area between home plate and the three bases is diamond-shaped.

Baseball history goes back to the mid-1800s. In all that time, one thing is certain. As long as the game of baseball has been played, baseball nicknames have been made.

CHAPTER 1

Hitters

There are all kinds of nicknames for hitting a baseball. A "chopper" is a high-bouncing grounder. A "bleeder" is a weakly hit ball to the outfield. A "blooper" is a fly ball that lands just between infielders and outfielders. Home runs are "dingers," "taters," "moon shots," and "round-trippers." You can bet that the following nicknamed hitters could all "tear the cover off the ball."

MIKE TROUT:
The Millville Meteor

Mike Trout is one of the best all-around players in Major League Baseball (MLB). He backs up his greatness with awards. The Los Angeles Angels slugger won the American League **MVP** in 2014, 2016, and 2019. The speedy centerfielder is called The Millville Meteor. His hometown is Millville, New Jersey.

Mike Trout was drafted in 2009 and won American League Rookie of the Year in 2012.

JOSÉ BAUTISTA:
Joey Bats

José Bautista easily earned the nickname Joey Bats. The outfielder led the American League in home runs in 2010 and 2011. He crushed 344 homers over a 15-year career. After hitting homers, Joey Bats sometimes celebrated by flipping his bat. **Opponents** did not like to see him toss bats, but Bautista's fans sure did.

Giancarlo "Bigfoot" Stanton joined the Yankees in 2018 after playing his first 8 seasons with the Marlins.

GIANCARLO STANTON:
Bigfoot

Giancarlo Stanton put up big numbers in 2017. He hit 59 homers and had 132 **RBI**s. He won the American League MVP. But Stanton is more than just big numbers. At 6-foot-6 (198 centimeters), Stanton is a big guy. It's easy to see why teammates started calling him Bigfoot back when he played in the **minor leagues**.

CHRISTIAN YELICH: Yeli

MLB started Players' Weekend in 2017. Teams wear special uniforms during the weekend's games. Players get to choose a nickname for the back of their jersey. Yeli was the simple nickname Milwaukee Brewers star Christian Yelich picked. Yelich won the National League MVP in 2018. He also led the league in batting average two years in a row.

BRYCE HARPER:
Bam Bam

Bryce Harper's parents called him Bam Bam when he was a kid. Harper has two middle names, Aron and Max. His initials spell out B.A.M. There's also a character named Bamm-Bamm from a classic TV cartoon called *The Flintstones*. Bamm-Bamm was super strong and carried a club. That club is kind of like the bat that Harper uses to smash home runs.

Diamond Fact

The game show *Jeopardy!* once featured Bryce Harper's nickname. The answer: In 2015 this Washington Nationals outfielder nicknamed "Bam Bam" hit 42 home runs and was the NL MVP. The question: Who is Bryce Harper?

"Bam Bam" Bryce Harper joined the Phillies in 2019. He played the first seven seasons of his pro career with the Nationals.

David Ortiz played 14 seasons with the Boston Red Sox.

DAVID ORTIZ: Big Papi

David Ortiz led the Boston Red Sox to World Series titles in 2004, 2007, and 2013. Boston teammates called the slugger "Papi," which means "daddy" in Spanish. The "big" part was added by TV sportscaster Jerry Remy. He asked Ortiz if he could call him "Big Papi." Ortiz, who is 6-foot-3 (191 cm) and 230 pounds (104 kilograms), said he wouldn't mind.

PETE ROSE: Charlie Hustle

As a **rookie** Pete Rose was given the nickname Charlie Hustle. Pitcher Whitey Ford didn't like it when Rose ran to first base after being walked. Ford came up with the name to tease the rookie. But Rose, who did everything at full speed, enjoyed the name. Charlie Hustle went on to collect more hits than anyone in major league history.

"Shoeless" Joe Jackson did wear shoes when he played (most) games.

"Shoeless" JOE JACKSON

Joe Jackson once played a game in his socks. He said his shoes were too tight to play in. Though he said he only did it once, he was called Shoeless Joe forever after. Jackson hit .356 in 13 major league seasons. Later, he was banned from baseball. He was accused of taking money to lose the 1919 World Series.

BEST OF THE REST: Other Great Hitter Nicknames

Steve "**Bye Bye**" Balboni

Frank Thomas: **The Big Hurt**

Harmon Killebrew: **Killer**

Stan "**The Man**" Musial

Adrian "**Cap**" Anson

CHAPTER 2

Pitchers

Cy Young pitched for 22 years in the major leagues.

Pitchers throw many different kinds of pitches. Those pitches also have nicknames. A fastball is called a "heater." A curveball is a "bender," "hook," or "Uncle Charlie." A pitch that hits a batter is a "beanball." Those nicknames are just for the pitches. What about the players who throw them?

"Dizzy" and "Daffy" Dean

In the 1930s, brothers Dizzy and Daffy Dean both played for the St. Louis Cardinals. In 1934 they helped their team win the World Series. Dizzy was older, and his real name was Jay. He was called Dizzy because it fit his wild and crazy attitude. Paul was two years younger and shy. He went by Daffy, just to go along with his big brother.

DENTON TRUE "Cy" YOUNG

Since 1956 the best pitchers in the major leagues win the Cy Young Award. The award is named after Cy Young, whose real name was Denton. Cy was short for **Cyclone**. People said he looked like a cyclone as he wound up and pitched. Young had 511 career wins. That's the most of any pitcher in history.

Diamond Fact

From 1891 to 1904, Cy Young won more than 20 games each season. In five of those seasons, he won 30 or more.

NOLAN RYAN:
The Ryan Express

Nolan Ryan was named "The Ryan Express" by media. They were referencing a 1965 movie with a similar name. Ryan pitched for 27 seasons in the major leagues, starting in 1966. He is the all-time leader in both strikeouts and walks.

Clayton Kershaw broke into the majors with the L.A. Dodgers in 2008.

CLAYTON "The Claw" KERSHAW

Clayton Kershaw won the Cy Young Award three times. He also won league MVP in 2014 with a 21–3 **record**. The strong left-hander gets his nickname from combining his first and last names. In 2020 he helped the Los Angeles Dodgers win the World Series.

MAX SCHERZER:
Mad Max

"Mad Max" Scherzer's nickname comes from how hard he plays. He's led the league in strikeouts three times. Mad Max is one of only six pitchers in MLB history to throw two no-hitters in a season. He has won the Cy Young Award in both the American League and the National League.

NOAH SYNDERGAARD: Thor

Thor is a superhero with long blond hair. He holds a hammer that can call down thunder and lightning. The likeness between Thor and New York Mets pitcher Noah Syndergaard is strong. Syndergaard was tied with three other pitchers in the league for most complete games in 2018.

Diamond Fact
Noah Syndergaard has worn a glove with the name Thor stitched into it while on the mound.

Noah Syndergaar appeared with the Mets in the 2015 World Series.

BEST OF THE REST: Other Great Pitcher Nicknames

Corey Kluber: **Klubot**

Jake Arrieta: **The Snake**

Walter "**The Big Train**" Johnson

Mariano "**The Sandman**" Rivera

Dwight "**Doc**" Gooden

CHAPTER 3

Fielders

Mookie Betts won his first Gold Glove award for his great outfield play in 2016.

Fielders are an important part of the game. They "turn two," or make double plays. They "scoop dirt," or snag ground balls. They make "snow cone" catches. They put baserunners in a "pickle." They wow us right and left—and most often in center!

MARKUS LYNN
"Mookie" BETTS

Many people think Mookie Betts's nickname comes from former player Mookie Wilson. Wilson was a star with the New York Mets in the 1980s. But Betts's parents say their son's nickname has to do with their love of Mookie Blaylock. Blaylock was a former NBA point guard.

Either way, Betts is an outstanding centerfielder. He won five Gold Glove Awards from 2016 to 2020. He was named American League MVP in 2018.

Ty Cobb won 12 American League batting titles during his pro career. He played from 1905–1928.

OZZIE SMITH:
The Wizard

Shortstop Ozzie Smith seemed to do magic as he scooped up ground balls. He made it look like the ball disappeared into his glove, hence his nickname the "Wizard." Ozzie Smith did more than dazzle fans with his glove. For special occasions, such as Opening Day, he would do a backflip as he took the field.

TY COBB: The
Georgia Peach

Ty Cobb's nickname, The Georgia Peach, brings to mind sweetness. But Cobb was rough and tough on the field. Cobb slid into bases with his spikes aimed high. He tried to hurt the fielder. He jawed with umps. He fought with teammates and coaches. But the Georgia native was a peach in the field and at the plate. Many consider him one of the best—and meanest—guys to ever take the diamond.

BEST OF THE REST: Other Great Fielder Nicknames

Francisco Lindor: **Mr. Smile**

Nolan Arenado: **The Sandblaster**

Yadier Molina: **Yadi**

Ken Griffey Jr.: **The Kid**

Brooks Robinson: **The Human Vacuum Cleaner**

CHAPTER 4

The Negro Leagues

Jackie Robinson first took the field for the Brooklyn Dodgers on April 15, 1947. That broke Major League Baseball's color line. Before that, Black players were not allowed in the major leagues. But Black baseball players had been playing in other leagues for many years before that. In 1920 the Negro National League was started, and rival leagues soon joined. The Negro Leagues was filled with players with All-Star nicknames.

Satchel Paige was famous for his powerful fastball.

LEROY "Satchel" PAIGE

One of the truly great pitchers in the history of baseball was Leroy "Satchel" Paige. He played for many teams in his long career, but he pitched the most for the Pittsburgh Crawfords. After Jackie Robinson broke Major League Baseball's color line in 1947, Paige was at last signed to a MLB contract. He made his debut with Cleveland in 1948 as a 42-year-old. He went on to pitch in parts of six seasons in the majors.

JAMES "Biz" MACKEY

James "Biz" Mackey was a catcher who talked a lot. News reporters said Mackey talked so much to hitters that he was "giving them the business." Mackey played and managed from 1918 to 1947. The teams he played on included the Hilldale Giants, Philadelphia Stars, and Newark Eagles.

ERNIE BANKS: **Mr. Cub**

At age 19, Ernie Banks started with the Kansas City Monarchs. But his nickname came from the MLB team he joined in 1953. No player wore the blue hat with a red C for more games than Banks. Mr. Cub played 2,528 games with the Chicago Cubs. He led all of the major leagues in homers twice and smashed 512 in his career.

Ernie Banks played in the Negro Leagues before he joined MLB's Chicago Cubs.

MAMIE "Peanut" JOHNSON

Three women played baseball in the Negro Leagues. Mamie Johnson was one of them. A 5-foot-3 (160 cm) pitcher, she once faced a hitter named Hank Baylis. He said she didn't look any bigger than a peanut. Johnson struck out Baylis and earned herself the nickname Peanut. Her pitching record in the Negro Leagues was 33 wins and 8 losses.

JAMES THOMAS
"Cool Papa" BELL

James Bell was one of the fastest players who ever laced up baseball cleats. Bell played in the Negro Leagues from 1922–1950, and he died in 1991. But tales of his speed live on. He once scored from first base on a bunt. He could flip a light switch and jump in bed before the room got dark. He got his nickname from a coach who noted how cool Bell was under pressure.

BEST OF THE REST: Other Great Negro League Nicknames

"Bullet Joe" Rogan

"Gentleman Dave" Malarcher

Sam "The Jet" Jethroe

Arthur "Rats" Henderson

Ted "Double Duty" Radcliffe

Josh Gibson: The Black Babe Ruth

George "Mule" Suttles

Wilson "Frog" Redus

"Candy Jim" Taylor

CHAPTER 5

Hall of Famers

BABE THE PITCHER

Many fans today know Babe Ruth for his hitting. But before Ruth became an outstanding hitter, he was at his best as a pitcher. In his first six seasons as a major leaguer, Babe Ruth pitched 158 games for the Boston Red Sox. Once he pitched a 13-inning shutout. After he went to the Yankees in 1920, he only pitched in five more games for the rest of his career. In the field for the Yankees, Ruth usually played right or left field.

Baseball is a grand old game. Its best players often earn a place in the Baseball Hall of Fame. Many of those baseball greats also have great nicknames.

GEORGE HERMAN
"Babe" RUTH

George Herman Ruth was so famous that his most well-known nickname, Babe, wasn't enough. He was also called The Bambino, The Sultan of Swat, and The Colossus of Clout, as well as others.

Ruth hit homers at an amazing rate. From 1918 to 1931, he led the American League in dingers 12 times. He was part of the first group to enter the Hall of Fame in 1936.

Reggie Jackson was known for his for his legendary playoff performances.

"Yogi" BERRA

Lawrence Peter "Yogi" Berra was one of the greatest catchers of all-time. He was nicknamed by a childhood friend. Jack Maguire decided to call Berra "Yogi" after the two watched a movie. The movie had a person who practiced yoga that looked like Berra. Yogi Berra was a three-time MVP with the Yankees and made the Hall of Fame in 1972.

"Joltin'" JOE DIMAGGIO

In the 1930s and 1940s, "Joltin'" Joe DiMaggio was the crown jewel of the Yankees **dynasty**. DiMaggio was also known as the Yankee Clipper. In various seasons he led the American League in batting average, home runs, and runs batted in. He was also AL MVP three different times, in 1939, 1941, and 1947. He entered the Hall of Fame in 1955.

REGGIE JACKSON:
Mr. October

The World Series is most often held in October. And this was Reggie Jackson's time to shine. Jackson stood out in the 1977 World Series. Facing the Dodgers in Game 6, Jackson hit three straight home runs on the very first pitch each time—off three different pitchers! Mr. October entered the Hall of Fame in 1993.

Henry Aaron "hammered" pitches when he was up to bat.

HENRY AARON:
Hammerin' Hank

Henry Aaron broke Babe Ruth's record in 1974 to become, at that time, the all-time MLB record holder in career home runs. Hammerin' Hank hit a grand total of 755 home runs from 1954 to 1976. He was a 25-time All-Star and entered the Hall of Fame in 1982.

TED WILLIAMS: The
Splendid Splinter

The Splendid Splinter nickname belonged to Boston Red Sox outfielder Ted Williams. A splinter is a piece of wood, and the word refers to the wooden bat that Williams swung. To this day, Williams is the last player to hit for a batting average of .400 or better. Williams hit .406 in 1941. He joined the Hall of Fame in 1966.

LOYAL TO TEAM AND COUNTRY

Ted Williams was loyal to the Red Sox, playing all 19 of his major league seasons for Boston. Williams was also loyal to his country. He missed three seasons of baseball in his mid-20s while serving in the United States military. In 1952 and 1953, Williams was called to serve again. He flew 39 missions as a Marine pilot in the Korean War.

ROBERTO CLEMENTE: Arriba

"Arriba, arriba! Ándale, ándale!" means "Go, go! Come on, come on!" When Pirates outfielder Roberto Clemente came up to the plate with runners on base, fans cheered. They would shout "Arriba!" This became Clemente's nickname. Sadly, Clemente died in a plane crash in 1972 at age 38. He was voted into the Hall of Fame in 1973.

Roberto Clemente was an All-Star 15 times.

Diamond Fact

Baseball has two Hammerin' Hanks in the Hall of Fame. "Hammerin' Hank" Greenberg led the league in homers four times and was voted MVP twice. He was elected to the Hall of Fame in 1956.

BEST OF THE REST:
Other Great Hall of Famer Nicknames

Rod Carew: **Sir Rodney**

Willie Stargell: **Pops**

Willie Mays: **The Say Hey Kid**

Mickey Mantle: **The Mick**

Lou Gehrig: **The Iron Horse**

CHAPTER 6

The Wild and Weird

Each time he was up to bat, Mike Hargrove went through a series of moves.

Some plays made on the field have weird nicknames. The "can of corn" is an easy fly ball to catch. A "dying quail" is a batted ball that seems to fall suddenly, wounded, out of the sky. Pitchers "nibble" around the "plate" when they throw pitches close to, but not in, the strike zone. Some of the nicknames players earn are just plain weird as well.

MIKE HARGROVE:
The Human Rain Delay

Mike Hargrove really took his time when he stepped up to the plate. Did someone put itching powder in his uniform? Did his uniform not fit right? Was he feeling okay? It was hard to tell. Hargrove scratched. He shrugged. He stretched. He tapped his bat on his cleats. He checked his equipment, over and over and over again. It seemed like the game was in a rain delay.

MORDECAI "Three Finger" BROWN

Athletes who suffer injuries sometimes have to quit playing. Mordecai Brown actually turned an injury into a good thing. Brown lost two of his fingers and hurt his pitching hand in a farm accident. But he found a new way to grip the baseball. "Three Finger" Brown won more than 20 games each season between 1906 and 1911.

MATT STAIRS:
Wonder Hamster

Matt Stairs had a few nicknames in his 19 seasons of major league baseball. He played for 12 different teams, including with the Oakland A's from 1996 to 2000. Wonder Hamster was a nickname given to him by a fan in Oakland. He was also called Professional Hitter.

Slugger Matt Stairs had a couple of different nicknames.

BILL KEISTER:
Wagon Tongue

Bill Keister wasn't the best shortstop. In fact, he set the major league record for worst fielding average in 1901. But he could talk. And talk. And talk. And talk. His teammates rewarded him with the name Wagon Tongue.

ELTON "Ice Box" CHAMBERLAIN

When the game was on the line, Elton Chamberlain was such a cool pitcher that he was given the name Ice Box. He played for the Louisville Colonels, St. Louis Browns, and Cincinnati Reds in the 1890s.

Elton Chamberlain pitched from 1886 to 1896.

Diamond Fact

Ice Box Chamberlain could pitch with either arm. In some games, when one arm got tired, he would switch to the other.

Willie Keeler may have been small, but he made up for it with his skills at the plate.

"Wee Willie" KEELER

Also nicknamed "Hit 'Em Where They Ain't," Willie Keeler was one of the smaller players on the diamond. Standing 5-foot-4 (163 cm) and weighing 140 pounds (64 kg), Wee Willie starred for teams in New York, Brooklyn, and Baltimore. In 1897 with the Baltimore Orioles, he hit an amazing .424 over 129 games.

. . . .

The sport of baseball has been full of great nicknames for many years. What amazing players and their nicknames will step up to the plate in the future?

BEST OF THE REST: Other Great Wild and Weird Nicknames

William **Pickles** Dillhoefer

Bill "**Spaceman**" Lee

Russ Meyer: **Mad Monk**

Tom "**Flash**" Gordon

Dennis "**Oil Can**" Boyd

George "**Sparky**" Anderson

Jimmy Wynn: **Toy Cannon**

Ron Cey: **The Penguin**

Luke Appling: **Old Aches and Pains**

Joe Medwick: **Ducky**

GLOSSARY

cyclone (SY-clohn)—a storm with strong winds that blow around a center

dynasty (DYE-nuh-stee)—a team that wins multiple championships over a period of several years

minor league (MYE-nur LEEG)—a group of professional baseball teams where athletes play to prepare for a major league team

MVP (EM-vee-pea)—an award that goes to the best player in a game or season; MVP stands for Most Valuable Player

opponent (uh-POH-nuhnt)—a person or team who competes against another person or team

RBI (AR-bee-eye)—runs batted in

record (REK-urd)—when something is done better than anyone has done it before; also a collection of facts

rookie (RUK-ee)—a first-year player

READ MORE

Chandler, Matt. *Baseball's Greatest Walk-Offs and Other Crunch-Time Heroics.* North Mankato, MN: Capstone, 2020.

Murray, Hallie. *Satchel Paige: Legendary Pitcher.* New York: Enslow Publishing, 2020.

Rajczak, Michael. The *Greatest Baseball Players of All Time.* New York: Gareth Stevens Publishing, 2019.

INTERNET SITES

MLB Players
mlb.com/players

Negro Leagues History
nlbm.com/negro-leagues-history

Sports Illustrated Kids: Baseball
sikids.com/baseball

INDEX